LE CORDON BLEU

HOME COLLECTION

SUMMER

PERIPLUS
EDITIONS

contents

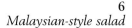

recipe ratings 🕸 *easy* 🕸🕸 *a little more care needed* 🕸🕸🕸 *more care needed*

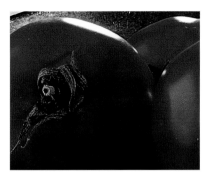

Gazpacho

Of Arabic origin, the name of this soup means "soaked bread." Gazpacho originates from Seville in the south of Spain, but many Spanish regions have their own versions of the soup.

Preparation time 35 minutes + 2 hours refrigeration
Total cooking time None
Serves 6–8

GAZPACHO
1 cup fine fresh white bread crumbs
2 tablespoons red wine vinegar
2 cloves garlic
3/4 English cucumber, unpeeled and coarsely chopped
1 onion, chopped
1/2 green bell pepper, coarsely chopped
10 ripe tomatoes, quartered and seeded
1/2 cup olive oil

TO GARNISH
1/4 English cucumber, unpeeled
1/2 green bell pepper
4 slices of bread, crusts removed and toasted

1 In a food processor or blender, place the bread crumbs, vinegar, garlic, cucumber, onion, bell pepper, tomatoes and a teaspoon of salt. Purée and then push through a metal strainer.

2 Return to the food processor or blender and, with the machine running, pour in the olive oil in a thin steady stream. Alternatively, pour the mixture into a large bowl and briskly stir or whisk in the oil.

3 Check the flavoring, season with salt and freshly ground black pepper and add a little more vinegar if required for a refreshing tang. Check the consistency— the soup should be thin, so you may need to add a little more water to dilute it. Cover the bowl with two layers of plastic wrap and chill in the refrigerator for at least 2 hours.

4 To prepare the garnish, cut the bell pepper and bread into small cubes and place, with the cucumber, into individual small bowls.

5 Pour the soup into well-chilled bowls and pass around the bell peppers, croutons and cucumber for each person to sprinkle onto their own soup.

Chef's tips To serve, you could add two or three ice cubes to chill the soup, or for more color, chop a red bell pepper along with the green.

Make the soup a day in advance for a mature, well-rounded flavor, but cover it well, because the soup has a strong odor that can affect other foods in the refrigerator.

Malaysian-style salad

Tangy, sweet and crisp, this salad makes a delightful accompaniment to many Asian dishes.
Try using a variety of fruits and vegetables such as mangoes, grapefruit, carambola (star fruit) or cucumber.

Preparation time **40 minutes + 1 hour 10 minutes**
  standing
Total cooking time **5 minutes**
Serves 6–8 people as a side dish

VINAIGRETTE
1–2 fresh red chiles
1 tablespoon brown sugar or honey
1/4 cup rice vinegar
1 tablespoon sesame oil
1 teaspoon light soy sauce (see Chef's tip)
1 teaspoon finely grated peeled fresh ginger root

1 medium ripe pineapple, peeled and trimmed
2 carrots
2 kiwi fruit
1 yellow bell pepper
1 red bell pepper
2 cups trimmed snow peas
1 tablespoon shredded coconut

1 To make the vinaigrette, thinly slice or coarsely chop the chiles. Place them in a nonreactive bowl or jar and add the sugar or honey, rice vinegar, sesame oil, soy sauce and ginger. Mix well and check the seasoning. Set aside at room temperature for at least 1 hour, or refrigerate overnight. Stir or shake occasionally.

2 Cut the pineapple into six to eight wedges. Remove and discard the core, then cut each wedge into 1/2-inch pieces. Slice the carrots at an angle to the same size as the pineapple. Peel the kiwi fruit, cut in half lengthwise, then cut into 1/4-inch slices. Cut the bell peppers into bite-sized chunks.

3 Bring 2 quarts water to a boil. Salt the water well, then blanch the snow peas for about 90 seconds. Rinse well with cold water and drain. Cut the snow peas in half at an angle, to the size of the other vegetables.

4 Reserve some shredded coconut for the garnish; mix the remainder into the vinaigrette and soak for 5–10 minutes. Toss the fruit and vegetables together in a large bowl with the vinaigrette. Sprinkle with the reserved coconut and serve immediately.

Chef's tip Light soy sauce is paler and milder than regular soy sauce, and is preferred in some recipes because it will not affect the color and flavor of the dish. If it is hard to find, use 1/2 teaspoon salt instead.

Crab fritters with lime and ginger chutney

These warm crab and herb fritters are served with a tangy chutney which may be made well in advance.
They could also be served with a dipping sauce made of mayonnaise, yogurt and lime.

Preparation time **50 minutes + cooling**
Total cooking time **1 hour 10 minutes**
Makes about 12

LIME AND GINGER CHUTNEY
4 limes
juice of 1/2 lemon
juice of 1 orange
1 onion, sliced
1 clove garlic, crushed
1 tablespoon grated peeled fresh ginger root
pinch of saffron threads or powder
1 bay leaf
2–3 whole cloves
1/3 cup white wine vinegar
1/3 cup firmly packed brown sugar
1/2 cup golden raisins soaked in 1 tablespoon brandy
1 teaspoon tomato paste

CRAB FRITTERS
2–2 1/2 cups fresh bread crumbs
1/2 lb. skinned white fish fillets, such as brook trout, lingcod or haddock
1 egg white
1/3 cup heavy cream
1/2 lb. cooked white crabmeat, shredded
1/2 cup chopped mixed fresh herbs, such as dill, chives, parsley and tarragon
oil, for deep-frying

1 To make the lime and ginger chutney, peel the limes and remove the pith using a small sharp knife. Cut the limes into segments by making an incision on both sides of each membrane towards the center of the fruit, lifting out each lime segment as you work. Set aside. Squeeze the remaining juice from the empty membranes, add it to the lemon and orange juice and place in a saucepan with all the chutney ingredients except the lime segments. Simmer for 45–55 minutes, or until the mixture is almost dry, stirring frequently. Allow to cool slightly, then add the lime segments and set aside to allow to cool completely.

2 Sprinkle the bread crumbs onto a sheet of waxed paper. To make the crab fritters, purée the fish in a food processor. Add the egg white, season with salt and pepper, and process again until well blended. Using the pulse button or an on/off action, carefully add the cream—do not overprocess or it will separate.

3 Transfer the mixture to a bowl, then place the bowl in a larger bowl of ice. Using a large metal spoon or plastic spatula, fold in the crabmeat and mixed herbs. Using two tablespoons, shape the mixture into small ovals about 2 x 1 1/4 inches in size. Gently roll in the bread crumbs to coat, using the paper to help toss the crumbs and to avoid handling the mixture.

4 Preheat a deep-fat fryer or deep saucepan, one-third full of oil, to 325°F. The oil is the right temperature when a cube of bread dropped into the oil browns in 30 seconds. Cook the fritters in batches for 4–6 minutes, or until golden brown all over, turning with a long-handled metal spoon. Drain on crumpled paper towels. Season with salt and serve warm with the chutney.

Chef's tips Once shaped and coated, the fritters can be refrigerated for up to 24 hours before deep-frying.

The chutney can be served as soon as it has cooled, or it may be left to mature for up to 2 weeks in an airtight container in the refrigerator. You can also serve this chutney with cold meat, terrines or pâtés.

Caesar salad

This salad is often thought of as an American dish, but was actually created by Caesar Cardini in Tijuana, Mexico in the 1920s.

Preparation time **20 minutes**
Total cooking time **15 minutes**
Serves 4

DRESSING
2 egg yolks
I tablespoon lemon juice, or to taste
2/3 cup olive oil
4 anchovy fillets, finely chopped
2 cloves garlic, finely chopped

2 eggs
I head of romaine lettuce
4 slices of white bread, crusts removed
1/3 cup olive oil
1/3 cup freshly grated Parmesan
2 tablespoons finely chopped fresh parsley

1 To make the dressing, beat the egg yolks and lemon juice using a whisk or an electric blender. Add the oil in a thin steady stream and beat until thick and smooth. Stir in the anchovies and garlic and season to taste with salt, pepper and extra lemon juice. Set aside.

2 To hard-cook the eggs, place them in a small saucepan and cover with cold water. Bring to a gentle boil and cook for 10 minutes. Drain and cool in cold water, then peel and chop finely.

3 Tear the lettuce into bite-sized pieces and set aside in the refrigerator. To make the croutons, cut the bread into even cubes. Heat the oil in a skillet and brown the bread until nicely golden. Remove and drain on crumpled paper towels.

4 In a large serving bowl, toss the lettuce in the dressing. Sprinkle with the remaining ingredients to serve.

Chef's tip To make the salad a meal in itself, try adding smoked duck breast, chicken or salmon.

Shrimp salad with lime mayonnaise

To make the most of the natural flavors of this chilled salad, season with a light hand. A touch of cumin and a refreshing lime mayonnaise transforms a simple lunch into a taste of summer.

Preparation time 15 minutes + 30 minutes standing
Total cooking time None
Serves 6

❋

I cucumber
2 tablespoons salt
I tablespoon cumin seeds, lightly toasted (see Chef's tip)
I lb. peeled cooked shrimp, deveined, drained and dried
juice and finely grated rind of I lime
¹/2 cup plain yogurt
¹/2 cup mayonnaise
sprigs of fresh chervil, to garnish

1 Peel the cucumber, cut it in half lengthwise and use a teaspoon to scrape out the seeds. Cut the flesh into long, thin strips, about 4 inches by ¹/8 inch. Place on a large plate, sprinkle with the salt and let stand for 30 minutes. (The salt will bring out the water and concentrate the flavor.) Drain off the liquid, pat dry with paper towels and sprinkle with the cumin seeds.

2 Place the shrimp in a bowl, add 1 or 2 teaspoons of lime juice to taste and stir to combine. Season to taste with salt and freshly ground pepper. Firmly pack the shrimp into six individual soufflé or custard cups, then set aside in the refrigerator.

3 In a small bowl, mix together the grated lime rind, yogurt, mayonnaise and remaining lime juice to taste. Stir together until well combined.

4 To serve, turn out the molds onto six chilled plates. Arrange the cucumber strips around the shrimp, and drizzle some lime and yogurt mayonnaise around. Sprinkle a little salt over the shrimp if desired. Garnish with a sprig of chervil and serve chilled.

Chef's tip To toast cumin seeds, place them in a dry skillet. Fry over moderate heat for about 2 minutes, or until fragrant, taking care not to let the seeds burn or they will become bitter.

Carpaccio with arugula and Parmesan

*Beef carpaccio is a classic Italian first course consisting of very thin slices of raw beef
served with a vinaigrette and often topped with onions, or capers as in this recipe.*

*Preparation time **15 minutes + 30 minutes freezing***
*Total cooking time **None***
Serves 4

3/4 lb. beef tenderloin steak (see Chef's tips)
3 tablespoons lemon juice
3 tablespoons extra virgin olive oil
3 oz. piece of Parmesan, at room temperature
3 cups washed, crisp arugula leaves
 or watercress sprigs
1/4 cup drained capers

1 To prepare the carpaccio, trim the beef well of fat
and sinew. Wrap tightly in plastic wrap and freeze for at
least 30 minutes, or until very firm but not rock-solid.
Remove the plastic wrap and using a very sharp, thin
knife, slice the meat as thinly as possible. Place each slice
between two layers of plastic wrap and lightly pound
the slices to flatten them.
2 Divide the beef among four plates, arranging the
slices in a single layer, overlapping them slightly. Cover
with plastic wrap and refrigerate until ready to serve.

3 To make the dressing, whisk together the lemon juice
and olive oil. Season to taste with salt and freshly
ground pepper and set aside.
4 Using a vegetable peeler, shave cheese curls from the
piece of Parmesan, allowing six shavings per plate. Set
aside until ready to use.
5 Just before serving, toss the arugula leaves or
watercress in half the dressing and arrange on the plates
with the carpaccio. Sprinkle with the Parmesan and
capers. Drizzle with the remaining dressing and serve at
once with freshly ground black pepper.

Chef's tips When making your own carpaccio, it is very
important to use a good-quality cut of very fresh meat.
Alternatively, for the thinnest possible slices of beef,
your butcher may be able to prepare the carpaccio for
you. Order the meat several days in advance for the day
you plan to serve it, and specify how you would like it
prepared. Ask your butcher to lay out the slices on a
sheet of plastic wrap for easier handling.

This recipe can be adjusted to taste by adding freshly
chopped herbs such as basil, as well as olives, anchovies
or roasted and skinned red bell peppers.

Mediterranean salad

Balsamic vinegar is an Italian vinegar that adds an exquisite flavor to this salad.

Preparation time **30 minutes**
Total cooking time **None**
Serves 4

⚜

DRESSING
1/3 cup balsamic vinegar
3/4 cup olive oil
4 cloves garlic, finely chopped
1/3 cup finely chopped fresh basil leaves

4 tomatoes
2 ripe avocados
1/4 lb. mozzarella cheese, thinly sliced
1/3 cup diced prosciutto

1 To make the dressing, pour the balsamic vinegar into a bowl and slowly whisk in the olive oil. Once the oil has been incorporated, mix in the finely chopped garlic and basil leaves and season with salt and freshly ground black pepper.
2 Using a sharp knife, remove the stem ends from the tomatoes. Slice the tomatoes into wedges and place in a large salad bowl. Dice the avocados into large cubes and add to the tomatoes. Add the mozzarella cheese slices and sprinkle with the diced prosciutto.
3 Add the dressing and gently mix together. Season to taste with salt and freshly ground pepper and serve at once with crusty bread.

Watercress salad

This is a refreshing salad with a light dressing that is simple and quick to prepare.

Preparation time **20 minutes + 1 hour refrigeration**
Total cooking time **None**
Serves 4

⚜

2 quarts washed, crisp watercress sprigs,
   stems removed
8–10 cherry tomatoes
1 1/2 cups feta cheese, cut into cubes
1 red onion, thinly sliced
1/3 cup green olives, pitted
1/3 cup black olives, pitted

DRESSING
2 cloves garlic, finely chopped
3 tablespoons lemon juice
3 tablespoons olive oil

1 Place all the salad ingredients in a large serving bowl. Cover and refrigerate for 1 hour, or until well chilled.
2 To make the dressing, whisk together all the dressing ingredients. Add to the salad, toss well, and season to taste with salt and freshly ground pepper.

Chef's tips Be careful when adding salt to this salad as the olives and feta cheese already contain a lot of salt.

When using raw onions in a salad, remember they are milder in summer and stronger in winter. If an onion seems too strong to use raw, soak the slices in salted water for about 30 minutes, then rinse well before using.

Mediterranean salad (bottom) with Watercress salad

Salade niçoise

Salade niçoise is a typical southern dish from Nice, usually containing tomatoes, tuna and black olives. Originally this salad did not include cooked vegetables, but as it began to appear on menus around France, local chefs made their own adaptations, including the addition of potatoes.

Preparation time **40 minutes + 20 minutes cooling**
Total cooking time **1 hour 20 minutes**
Serves 4

3/4 cup olive oil
I bay leaf
4 sprigs of fresh thyme
I piece of fresh tuna, about 3/4 lb., skin removed
10 oz. waxy or boiling potatoes
1/2 lb. green beans
3 tablespoons white wine vinegar
I green bell pepper, cut into julienne strips
  (see Chef's tip)
I red bell pepper, cut into julienne strips
2 red onions, thinly sliced
I butterhead lettuce, such as bibb or Boston
4 tomatoes, cut into quarters
4 hard-cooked eggs, peeled and quartered
13/4 oz. can anchovy fillets, drained
30 black olives

1 Preheat the oven to 300°F. In a small flameproof baking pan, place the oil, bay leaf, thyme and tuna. Warm over low heat for 5 minutes, then place in the oven for 30 minutes, or until the tuna feels firm. Allow to cool for 20 minutes in the oil, remove the tuna and place on a rack to drain. Strain the oil and set aside.

2 Put the unpeeled potatoes in cold, salted water. Bring to a boil and cook for 30–35 minutes, or until the tip of a knife easily pierces them. Remove from the water and allow to cool. Peel, then slice into thick rounds.

3 Trim the beans and cook in boiling salted water for 8 minutes, or until tender. Refresh in cold water and drain.

4 To make the vinaigrette, whisk the vinegar and some salt together, then gradually whisk in the reserved oil.

5 Toss the potatoes, green beans, bell peppers and onions with a little vinaigrette and season to taste with salt and black pepper. Break the tuna into bite-sized pieces and mix with some of the vinaigrette. Arrange a few leaves of lettuce on each plate. In the center, place a mound of the potatoes. Top with the green beans, bell peppers and onions and finish with the tuna. Alternate the tomato and egg quarters around the edge and finish with the anchovies and olives. Serve the remaining vinaigrette on the side or drizzle over the salad just before serving.

Chef's tip Julienne strips are strips of vegetables, the size and shape of matchsticks.

Pan-fried duck breast with citrus salad

The rich flavors of juicy duck are balanced perfectly in this dish by the refreshing bite of citrus. Although simple to prepare, this wonderful meal is worthy of special occasions.

*Preparation time **20 minutes***
*Total cooking time **35 minutes***
Serves 4

❂ ❂

2 oranges
2 grapefruit
1/2 cup sugar
5 tablespoons corn oil
1/4 cup vegetable oil
4 duck breasts, about 6 oz. each
I small head of radicchio
1/2 small curly endive
1/2 small oak or red leaf lettuce

1 Using a vegetable peeler, peel the rind from one orange and one grapefruit, avoiding the white pith. If there is any pith on the underside of the peel, remove it with a sharp knife to leave only the colored rind. Cut the rind into very fine shreds and place in a saucepan with enough cold water to cover well. Bring to a boil, reduce the heat and simmer for 1 minute. Drain.

2 In a small saucepan, dissolve the sugar in 1 cup water over low heat. Bring to a boil, then reduce the heat, add the shredded rind and simmer for 8 minutes, or until candied—it will be soft and sweet. Lift out with a fork and spread over an upturned metal strainer to drain and cool. Finely grate the rind of the remaining orange and grapefruit and set aside in a small bowl.

3 Using a small sharp knife, cut away the white pith from the two oranges and grapefruit. Cut the fruit into

segments by making an incision on both sides of each membrane towards the center of the fruit, lifting out each segment as you proceed. Set the segments aside. Squeeze 2–3 tablespoons of juice from the empty fruit membranes into the bowl with the grated rind. Slowly add the corn oil, whisking vigorously until the dressing has emulsified, then season to taste with salt and freshly ground pepper.

4 Heat the vegetable oil in a shallow skillet. Trim the fat from the duck breasts and make sure all the feather stubs have been removed. Cook the duck, skin-side-up, for 6–8 minutes, or until golden brown. Turn and cook the skin side for 10–15 minutes, or until the flesh is just pink. Remove from the saucepan and let rest in a warm place.

5 Drain the excess fat from the saucepan and allow the saucepan to cool slightly. Add the dressing to the saucepan, scraping well with a wooden spoon to mix in the saucepan juices.

6 Tear the salad leaves into bite-sized pieces and toss them in some of the dressing, then pile them to the side of each serving plate. Slice the duck into diagonal slices about 1/4 inch thick, and arrange the slices in a semicircle around the other edge of the plate. Arrange the fruit segments on the plate, spoon any remaining dressing over the duck and sprinkle with a little of the candied peel.

Chef's tips When available, use a pink grapefruit instead of one of the yellow grapefruit in this recipe. Pink grapefruit has a lovely flavor and color.

Dressed crab

In Britain, the most traditional way to enjoy fresh crab is to "dress" it. This enduring favorite is well worth the effort and evokes the feeling of an old-fashioned, English seaside holiday.

*Preparation time **40 minutes***
*Total cooking time **10 minutes***
Serves 1–2

2 eggs, at room temperature
1 cooked crab, about 1 1/2–2 lb.
  (see Chef's tips)
1–2 tablespoons mayonnaise, to taste
1 cup fresh bread crumbs
Worcestershire or Tabasco sauce, to taste
1/4 cup chopped fresh parsley
3 canned anchovy fillets, to garnish
3 teaspoons drained capers, to garnish
2 tablespoons sliced stuffed green olives, to garnish
4 slices whole wheat bread
1 tablespoon unsalted butter, at room temperature
1 lime or lemon, cut into wedges

1 To hard-cook the eggs, place them in a small saucepan and cover with cold water. Bring to a gentle boil and cook for 10 minutes. Drain and cool in cold water. Peel the eggs and push the whites and the yolks separately through a fine metal strainer.

2 Prepare the crab, following the method in the Chef's techniques on page 63. Scrape all the creamy brown meat from the shell and flake it into a bowl. Stir in the mayonnaise and bread crumbs to bind, adding more of each if the flavor of the dark meat is too strong. Season with salt, freshly ground pepper and Worcestershire or Tabasco sauce.

3 Crack open the claws and remove all the white meat, checking that there are no shell splinters left (see Chef's tips). Season to taste.

4 Place the white meat from the claws and body of the crab towards the two outer sides of the cleaned and dried shell. Spoon the brown meat into the center, then arrange the chopped parsley on the seams in between. Cover half of the white meat with the egg whites; spoon the egg yolks on the dark meat. Garnish with anchovies, capers and sliced olives. Butter the bread thinly, and serve the dressed crab with the bread and lime or lemon wedges to the side.

Chef's tips When choosing a crab, select one that feels heavier than it looks. If possible, buy a fresh crab, as frozen crabs lose a lot of flavor and liquid as they defrost. Male crabs have larger claws than females.

The best way to check there are no shell splinters in the meat is to throw pinches of the meat onto a baking sheet. Listen for the sound of shell pieces: if you do hear any, discard the meat.

Asian roast poussins

In this dish, an Asian-style marinade transforms delicately flavored baby chickens into something very special. Marinating them overnight will make them even more tender and succulent.

*Preparation time **45 minutes + overnight marinating***
*Total cooking time **40 minutes***
*Serves **4***

MARINADE
4 stalks fresh or dried lemongrass, white part only, halved
3/4 cup chopped fresh cilantro leaves, stems and roots
4 shallots, peeled and quartered
8 cloves garlic, peeled
1/3 cup peeled and chopped fresh ginger root
1/3 cup crushed jaggery (palm sugar) or lightly packed brown sugar
2 tablespoons curry powder
2 teaspoons ground black pepper
2 teaspoons salt
5 tablespoons fish sauce
2 cups canned unsweetened coconut milk

2 poussins (baby chickens), each 1 1/4–1 1/2 lb.
2 tablespoons oil

1 To make the marinade, very finely chop the lemongrass, cilantro, shallots, garlic and fresh ginger in a blender or small food processor. Add the sugar, curry powder, pepper, salt and fish sauce and process for 30 seconds. With the machine still running, add ½ cup of the coconut milk. Process until smooth, then transfer to a shallow, nonreactive bowl.

2 Cut the baby chickens in half and toss them in the marinade to coat well all over. Cover and refrigerate overnight, turning once or twice.

3 Preheat the oven to 450°F. Coat the bottom of a baking dish with the oil. Reserving the marinade, place the chickens in the dish and bake for 25–30 minutes, turning three or four times.

4 Transfer the reserved marinade to a saucepan and mix in the remaining coconut milk. Place over medium heat and bring to a gentle boil. Simmer for 5 minutes, then strain. Season to taste and keep warm. Serve the marinade over the chicken or on the side.

Chef's tip Cilantro stems have a more intense flavor than the leaves, and are often used for marinades.

Asparagus, artichoke and lobster salad

This is an elegant salad for a special occasion. The walnut oil adds a delicious nutty flavor to the dressing, but don't be tempted to increase the quantity because it has a strong flavor.

*Preparation time **1 hour + chilling***
*Total cooking time **35 minutes***
Serves 4

♦ ♦ ♦

COURT BOUILLON
I large carrot, thinly sliced
2 onions, thinly sliced
2 stalks celery, thinly sliced
I leek, white part only, thinly sliced
3 sprigs of fresh thyme
I bay leaf
10 black peppercorns
2 cups white wine
1/4 cup salt

3 uncooked lobster tails
24 stalks asparagus
1/3 cup salt, extra

DRESSING
1/4 cup sherry vinegar
I shallot, finely chopped
1/4 cup walnut oil
1/2 cup vegetable oil
I tablespoon chopped fresh chervil
   or chives

4 large artichoke hearts, from a jar or can
20 whole fresh chervil leaves, to garnish

1 To make the court bouillon, place all the vegetables with the thyme sprigs, bay leaf, peppercorns and wine in a large kettle or stockpot and bring to a boil. Cook for 5 minutes over high heat. Add the salt and 4 quarts water and return to a boil. Add the lobster tails, bring to a boil and cook for 12 minutes. Remove the pan from the heat and allow the lobster to cool slightly.

2 When the lobster is cool enough to handle, remove it from the bouillon. Discard the bouillon. Remove the tail flesh in a single piece, following the method in the Chef's techniques on page 63, then slice into medallions. Cover and refrigerate.

3 Wash the asparagus under cold, running water. Using a small knife, remove the spurs from the asparagus stalks, starting from the top and working down, then peel the outer layer from the lower two thirds of the stalk using a vegetable peeler. Lining up the tips, tie the stalks in bundles of six to eight, following the method in the Chef's techniques on page 63.

4 Bring 4 quarts water to a boil. Add the extra salt and then the asparagus bundles. Reduce the heat to a gentle simmer and cook for 5–8 minutes, or until the tips are tender. Remove the bundles and plunge into iced water, then drain on paper towels. Remove the strings, place in a bowl, cover and refrigerate.

5 To make the dressing, whisk together the vinegar and shallot. Gradually whisk in the oils, then the chervil or chives. Season and set aside. Rinse the artichokes well, pat dry, toss them in a little dressing and season to taste. Repeat with the asparagus, being careful not to break the tips. Refrigerate the vegetables until ready to use. To serve, arrange the artichokes, asparagus and lobster medallions on serving plates. Drizzle the remaining dressing around the artichokes, then garnish with the chervil leaves.

Chef's tip The cooked lobster tail shells can be frozen and used another time when preparing a seafood bisque or stock.

Shrimp with stir-fried bell peppers

This colorful dish is perfect as a starter or a light main course. It derives its superb flavor from the sweetness of the bell peppers, spiked with lemon oil and fresh ginger.

Preparation time **30 minutes + 1 hour infusion**
Total cooking time **5 minutes**
Serves 4

LEMON OIL
1/4 cup oil
finely grated rind of 1/4 lemon

2 1/2 lb. uncooked extra large or jumbo shrimp, with heads
    attached, if possible
1 red bell pepper
1 yellow bell pepper
1 tablespoon grated fresh peeled ginger root
1 tablespoon crushed garlic
1/4 cup dry sherry
2 tablespoons lemon juice
2 teaspoons light soy sauce

1 To make the lemon oil, gently warm the oil until lukewarm. Add the lemon rind, then allow the oil to cool and infuse for 1 hour. Strain before using.
2 Leaving the heads attached, remove the shells and tails from the shrimp. Remove the eyes. With a small knife, make a shallow cut along the back of each shrimp and carefully remove the dark vein. Pat the shrimp dry on paper towels.
3 Cut the bell peppers in half and remove the stems and seeds. Dice into 1/4-inch cubes and set aside.
4 Heat the lemon oil in a wok or deep heavy-bottomed skillet over high heat until it begins to smoke. Add the ginger, garlic and bell peppers and stir-fry for 1 minute, then add the shrimp and stir-fry for 1 minute more. Stir in the sherry, lemon juice and soy sauce and stir-fry for about 3 minutes, or until the shrimp are just tender. Serve the shrimp hot, with fresh crusty bread and a crisp green salad.

Cold ratatouille with chicken

Ratatouille is a French Provençal vegetable stew, originally from Nice. In this recipe it is served cold and is therefore best prepared the day before serving.

Preparation time **45 minutes + overnight refrigeration**
Total cooking time **1 hour 20 minutes**
Serves 4

RATATOUILLE
olive oil, for cooking
1 red bell pepper, cut into short strips
1 1/4 cups short strips of zucchini
1 1/4 cups short strips of eggplant
1 onion, chopped
2–3 tomatoes, peeled, seeded and chopped
2 cloves garlic, chopped
bouquet garni (see page 63)
1/4 cup chopped fresh basil

extra olive oil, for cooking
4 skinless chicken breast fillets
2 tablespoons lemon juice
1 sprig of fresh thyme

1 Preheat the oven to 300°F. To make the ratatouille, heat 1–2 tablespoons of oil in a deep, ovenproof skillet or Dutch oven. Sauté the bell pepper strips for 2–3 minutes over medium-high heat. Remove and drain on paper towels.

2 Add some more oil to the pan and sauté the zucchini and eggplant separately, adding oil as needed and removing the vegetables to drain on paper towels. Add the onion and cook without coloring over medium-low heat for 3–5 minutes, or until soft. Add the tomatoes and garlic and cook over low heat, stirring occasionally, for 3 minutes, or until the moisture evaporates.

3 Return the drained vegetables to the pan with the bouquet garni, then cover and bake for 30 minutes. Remove the bouquet garni, stir in the chopped basil and season to taste with salt and freshly ground black pepper. Allow to cool completely, then place in the refrigerator overnight.

4 Heat 2 tablespoons of oil over medium-low heat in a skillet. Season the chicken with salt and freshly ground pepper, then cook them in a single layer for about 5 minutes on each side, or until browned and just cooked through. Transfer to a wire rack to cool.

5 Drain the pan of excess oil and add the lemon juice with 1/2 cup water. Return to the heat and add the thyme. Stir well, scraping the base of the pan to dissolve the cooking juices. Transfer the sauce to a small saucepan and gently simmer for 10 minutes. Season to taste. Strain and set aside to cool.

6 To serve, divide the cold ratatouille among four plates, slice the chicken and arrange around the ratatouille. Drizzle the cooled sauce over the top.

Chef's tip If you are planning to serve a dish cold, season it well during cooking, as chilling can dull the flavors.

Lamb rib chops with pea fritters and garlic cream sauce

Lean pink lamb served with bright green pea fritters and a creamy garlic sauce make an unusual, appetizing and colorful summer's meal.

Preparation time 35 minutes + 40 minutes refrigeration
Total cooking time 1 hour
Serves 4

1 teaspoon salt
5 cups fresh shelled or frozen peas
2 teaspoons unsalted butter
1 egg yolk
2 teaspoons finely chopped fresh mint leaves
seasoned flour, for coating
2 eggs
2/3 cup dry bread crumbs
1/3 cup finely chopped blanched almonds
oil, for deep-frying
12 frenched lamb rib chops, trimmed of excess fat
2 tablespoons unsalted butter, melted

GARLIC CREAM SAUCE
10 cloves garlic, halved
1/3 cup white wine (not too dry)
1 1/4 cups heavy cream

1 Half-fill a medium saucepan with water and bring to a boil. Add the salt and peas, return to a boil, then reduce the heat and simmer for 3 minutes, or until the peas are tender. Drain well, then purée the peas in a food processor. Push the purée through a fine metal strainer to remove the skins.

2 Melt the butter in a skillet, add the pea purée and cook over low heat for about 7 minutes, or until the mixture is dry. Remove from the heat, stir in the egg yolk and chopped mint, and season with salt and freshly ground pepper. Allow to cool, then refrigerate for about 20 minutes, or until firm.

3 Place the seasoned flour on a sheet of waxed paper. Beat the eggs in a shallow dish. Mix together the bread crumbs and almonds and place them on another sheet of waxed paper. Divide the pea mixture into 12 portions and roll each portion between your palms into a ball, or shape them into patties. Coat the fritters with the flour, dip them in the beaten egg and then roll them in the almond mixture. Refrigerate for 20 minutes.

4 To make the garlic cream sauce, place the garlic in a small saucepan, cover with cold water and bring to a boil. Reduce the heat and simmer for 3 minutes, then drain. Return the garlic to the pan, add the white wine and cream, then cover and simmer gently for about 25 minutes, or until the garlic is soft. Pour the garlic mixture into a food processor or blender and process until smooth. Transfer to a clean pan to keep warm and season to taste. Preheat the broiler to high, and set the oven to its lowest setting.

5 Preheat a deep-fat fryer or deep saucepan, one-third full of oil, to 350°F. Deep-fry the fritters in small batches, stirring gently to make sure they brown evenly. When they are nicely golden, remove the fritters and drain on crumpled paper towels. Place on a wire rack and keep warm in the oven.

6 Brush the lamb chops with the melted butter and season with salt and freshly ground pepper. Broil for 3 minutes on each side for pink, or longer if preferred.

7 Divide the cutlets and fritters among warm serving plates and serve with a little garlic cream sauce.

Salmon with a shallot and cilantro vinaigrette

Here, a fresh salmon fillet is drizzled with a deliciously sharp vinaigrette, and for a light summery meal requires little more than a serving of new potatoes, or a crisp green salad.

*Preparation time **15 minutes***
*Total cooking time **20 minutes***
Serves 4

SHALLOT AND CILANTRO VINAIGRETTE
3 tablespoons white wine vinegar
2 shallots, finely chopped
I teaspoon coriander seeds, crushed
¹/3 cup white wine
I tablespoon dry vermouth
5 tablespoons fish stock
5 tablespoons olive oil
3 tomatoes, peeled, seeded and diced into
   ¹/4-inch cubes
²/3 cup chopped fresh cilantro leaves
I teaspoon lemon juice, or to taste

4 salmon fillets, about 6 oz. each
2 tablespoons unsalted butter

1 To make the shallot and cilantro vinaigrette, place the white wine vinegar, shallots and coriander seeds in a medium saucepan. Bring to a boil, then reduce the heat and simmer for 1 minute, or until reduced to a syrup. Add the wine and simmer for 3 minutes, or until reduced by two thirds. Stir in the vermouth and fish stock and simmer for 3 minutes, or until reduced by half. Season to taste, then remove from the heat and add the oil in a thin steady stream, whisking constantly until the sauce thickens and emulsifies. Strain and keep warm until ready to serve.

2 Season the salmon fillets on both sides with a little salt and freshly ground pepper. Melt the butter in a large skillet over medium heat, then cook the salmon for 4–5 minutes on each side, or until cooked through.

3 To serve, add the chopped tomatoes, cilantro leaves and lemon juice to the warm vinaigrette. Place each salmon fillet onto a hot serving plate and drizzle with some warm vinaigrette. If you like, sprinkle the salmon with a little chopped fresh dill or cilantro.

Chicken saté

Saté, an Indonesian dish, consists of skewered strips of marinated and broiled meat served with a smooth peanut sauce. Satés are a superb party snack, but make plenty as they disappear quickly!

Preparation time 35 minutes + 30 minutes soaking
  + 2 hours marinating
Total cooking time 40 minutes
Serves 6

MARINADE
1/2 teaspoon ground aniseed
1/2 teaspoon ground cumin
1 1/2 teaspoons ground turmeric
1 1/2 teaspoons ground coriander
2 shallots, chopped
1 clove garlic, finely chopped
1-inch piece fresh ginger root, finely chopped
2 stalks lemongrass, white part only, finely chopped
1/4 cup lightly packed brown sugar
5 tablespoons peanut oil
2 teaspoons soy sauce

6 skinless, boneless chicken breast halves

SATE SAUCE
1 clove garlic
2 tablespoons smooth peanut butter
2–3 tablespoons canned coconut milk
a few drops of Tabasco, or to taste
2 tablespoons honey
2 tablespoons lemon juice
2 tablespoons soy sauce

1 Soak 25 wooden skewers in water for 30 minutes. Combine all the marinade ingredients, mix thoroughly and set aside.

2 Cut the chicken into 1/4-inch strips and thread them onto the soaked skewers. Place in a shallow dish and thoroughly coat with the marinade. Cover and refrigerate for 2 hours.

3 To make the saté sauce, place the garlic in a small saucepan. Cover with water, bring to a boil, then reduce the heat and simmer for about 3 minutes. Refresh the garlic under cold water, drain well, then crush. Return the garlic to the pan with the peanut butter, coconut milk and 1/4 cup water, then stir over medium heat for 1–2 minutes, or until smooth and thick. Add all the remaining sauce ingredients and stir well until warmed through. If the sauce starts to separate, stir in a little water.

4 Preheat the broiler or barbecue grill to high. When hot, cook the chicken in batches for 5–6 minutes, turning three or four times. Remove and cover with foil while cooking the remaining chicken, then transfer to a serving platter. Serve the sauce separately.

Chef's tips Pre-packed ground spices tend to lose flavor during storage, so for special occasions you may like to grind your own. Simply fry the whole spices separately in a dry skillet, then process them in a food processor, or pound them into a powder using a mortar and pestle.

Seared tuna with chickpea salad

These tuna steaks are infused with Asian flavors and are seared quickly to great effect. The chickpea salad is very versatile, and is also lovely with broiled or barbecued vegetables or chicken.

Preparation time **10 minutes + overnight soaking + 3–4 hours marinating**
Total cooking time **1 hour 5 minutes**
Serves 4

2/3 cup dried chickpeas (garbanzos)
  (see Chef's tip)
4 tuna steaks, about 5–6 oz. each
1 bay leaf
1 shallot, chopped
1 small clove garlic, crushed
1 red chile, seeded and chopped
1 red bell pepper, chopped
1 avocado
2 tablespoons chopped fresh cilantro leaves
4 lime wedges, to serve

MARINADE
1/3 cup olive oil
finely grated rind and juice of 1 1/2 limes
6 stalks of fresh cilantro, coarsely chopped or
  slightly bruised

1 Soak the chickpeas overnight in plenty of cold water.
2 Combine the marinade ingredients and mix well. Place the tuna steaks in a shallow glass or nonreactive dish and pour in a third of the marinade, turning to coat both sides. Cover with plastic wrap and refrigerate for 3–4 hours, turning the tuna occasionally.
3 Drain the chickpeas and place in a large saucepan with enough water to cover. Add the bay leaf, bring to a boil, then reduce the heat and simmer for 1 hour, or until tender. Drain and set aside.
4 To make the chickpea salad, place the chickpeas, shallot, garlic, chile and bell pepper in a bowl and toss well. Peel and dice the avocado and fold into the salad with the cilantro. Strain the remaining marinade into the salad and season to taste.
5 Preheat the broiler or barbecue grill to high. When the broiler is hot, cook the tuna for about 2 minutes on each side, or grill for 1 minute on each side. Serve on warmed plates with a wedge of lime, and the chickpea salad on the side.

Chef's tip To save time, you can use 1½–2 cups canned chickpeas. Drain well and add to the salad in step 4.

Broiled lobster with a buttery Pernod sauce

Seafood gains a wonderful new dimension when served with a buttery sauce brightened with a dash of Pernod. The anise flavor of the sauce is enhanced with the infusion of star anise.

*Preparation time **15 minutes***
*Total cooking time **30 minutes***
Serves 4

PERNOD SAUCE
1 star anise
2 tablespoons Pernod
3/4 cup unsalted butter,
   cubed

4 uncooked lobster tails
3 tablespoons unsalted butter, melted

1 To make the Pernod sauce, place ½ cup water in a small saucepan with the star anise and bring to a boil. Reduce the heat to low and simmer for 10 minutes, or until reduced to about 2 tablespoons. Stir in half the Pernod. Whisking constantly, gradually add the butter, a few pieces at a time. Season with salt and ground white pepper, then place the pan in a bowl of hot water to keep warm or transfer the sauce to the top of a double boiler over hot water. (The sauce will separate if placed back over direct heat.)

2 Add the lobster tails to a large saucepan of boiling water and cook for 2 minutes, or until the shells turn bright orange. Drain and refresh in cold water. Place the lobster tails on a cutting board with the soft undershells facing down. Using a large knife, but without cutting all the way through, split the tails in half lengthwise down the back, then open them up.

3 Preheat the broiler to high. Brush the lobster flesh with the melted butter, season lightly, then broil, cut-side-down, for 5 minutes. Turn and broil the other side for 5–10 minutes, or until the flesh is firm. Transfer to serving plates. Stir the remaining Pernod into the sauce, then spoon a little sauce over the tails and serve the remainder on the side.

Chef's tip You could also use cooked whole Maine lobsters in this recipe. First remove the claws by twisting where they meet the body, then crack them using a nutcracker or meat mallet and set aside to serve later with the broiled lobsters.

Place the lobsters face-down on a cutting board. Using a large knife, but without cutting all the way through, split the lobsters in half lengthwise down the back, then open them up. Remove the vein along the tail, the small sac just behind the mouth, and any coral or grey-green liver (tomalley). Brush the flesh with melted butter, season lightly and broil under a hot broiler until heated through, turning during cooking.

Roast salmon with a basil and sweet pepper sauce

The smoky sweetness of roasted bell peppers marries with peppery basil in this inspirational sauce which makes salmon fillets, simply cooked, so sumptuous. Enjoy in the garden with a glass of chilled wine.

Preparation time **15 minutes**
Total cooking time **8–12 minutes**
Serves **4**

2 red bell peppers
1/3 cup olive oil
4 salmon fillets, about 6 oz. each, scaled but not skinned
2 tablespoons vegetable oil
2 tablespoons unsalted butter
2 tablespoons shredded fresh basil leaves

1 Preheat the oven to 425°F. Lightly brush the whole bell peppers with some olive oil, then place them on a baking sheet and roast for 15–20 minutes, or until the skin is blackened and blistered and the peppers are soft. Cover them with plastic wrap, or place in a plastic bag. (The peppers will sweat, making the skins peel off more easily.) Allow to cool. Peel away the skin, then halve and seed the bell peppers.

2 To make the sauce, place the peppers in a blender or food processor, add the remaining olive oil and process to a smooth purée. Season to taste with salt and freshly ground black pepper, and transfer to a small saucepan.

3 Season the salmon fillets with salt and freshly ground pepper. Heat the vegetable oil and butter in a roasting pan over high heat. Place the salmon in the pan, skin-side-up, then bake for 2 minutes. Turn and bake for 6 minutes, or until the salmon is cooked through and the skin is lightly colored.

4 Gently heat the sauce, then add the basil. Transfer the salmon to warm plates and pour the sauce around. Serve at once with a mixed green salad.

Teriyaki chicken

The name of this celebrated Japanese dish derives from the words "teri" meaning to shine, and "yaki" to broil. The chicken receives its appetizing glaze from the small quantity of sugar in the sauce.

*Preparation time **40 minutes***
*Total cooking time **35 minutes***
Serves 4

4 chicken leg and thigh quarters, boned
  (see page 62)
I tablespoon oil
I tablespoon chopped fresh cilantro

TERIYAKI SAUCE
1/3 cup sake (see Chef's tips)
1/3 cup mirin (see Chef's tips)
1/3 cup dark soy sauce
I tablespoon sugar
2 teaspoons finely chopped peeled fresh ginger root
I tablespoon finely chopped garlic

1 Using a fork, pierce the chicken through the skin several times to allow the sauce to penetrate, and to prevent shrinkage during cooking. In a large, deep skillet, heat a tablespoon of oil over medium-high heat. Brown the chicken, skin-side-down, for 3–5 minutes.

Reduce the heat to low, turn the chicken over, then cover and cook for 10 minutes. Transfer the chicken to a plate.

2 To make the teriyaki sauce, whisk together all the sauce ingredients until the sugar has dissolved. Pour into the skillet and bring to a boil. Whisking constantly, boil for 2–3 minutes, or until thickened slightly. Return the chicken to the pan and cook for about 15 minutes, or until the sauce has reduced to a glossy syrup. You will need to turn the chicken several times to completely coat it with the sauce.

3 To serve, slice the chicken and drizzle with any remaining sauce. Sprinkle the cilantro over the top.

Chef's tips Sake is a dry Japanese rice wine. Dry sherry can be used instead. Mirin is a mild sweet Japanese rice wine. If it is not available, you could use cider vinegar instead and increase the sugar by 1 tablespoon.

The chicken can be broiled or grilled, if you prefer. Marinate the chicken in the teriyaki sauce for at least 2 hours, then remove the chicken and boil the sauce for 2–3 minutes, or until thickened. Broil or grill the chicken, brushing it with the sauce.

Fish kebabs with
pumpkin and zucchini chutney

*These tangy, broiled mixed-fish kebabs are nicely complemented by a fresh-flavored chutney,
which is best made a day ahead to allow the flavors to mature. If there is a little chutney
to spare, try serving it with cheese or cold meats.*

*Preparation time **20 minutes + overnight refrigeration
+ 30 minutes soaking + 30 minutes marinating***
*Total cooking time **1 hour 20 minutes***
*Serves **4–6***

☼

PUMPKIN AND ZUCCHINI CHUTNEY
1 2/3 cups firm-fleshed pumpkin, finely chopped
1 2/3 cups zucchini, diced into 1/2-inch cubes
1 large onion, chopped
1 cup firmly packed brown sugar
1/3 cup white wine vinegar
1 tablespoon tomato paste

juice of 1/2 lemon
1 lb. salmon fillets, skinned
1 lb. swordfish or monkfish, skinned
juice of 1/2 lime
2 tablespoons chile oil (see Chef's tip)

1 To make the pumpkin and zucchini chutney, place
the pumpkin in a large, heavy-bottomed saucepan with
the zucchini, onion, sugar, vinegar, tomato paste and
1/3 cup water. Bring to a boil, stirring to dissolve the
sugar. Reduce the heat to low and simmer gently for
1 hour, or until soft and pulpy—the liquid should
evaporate, leaving enough syrup to keep the mixture
moist. Pour into a bowl to cool, then cover and
refrigerate overnight.

2 Place 12 wooden skewers in a shallow dish. Pour the
lemon juice over, adding a little cold water to just cover.
Let stand for 30 minutes and drain well.

3 Cut the fish into 3/4-inch cubes, then thread
alternately onto the skewers and place in a shallow
nonreactive dish. Combine the lime juice and chile oil
and pour over the kebabs, turning well to coat all sides.
Cover and refrigerate for 30 minutes.

4 Preheat the broiler to high. When hot, broil the
kebabs for 5–8 minutes on each side, or until light
golden and cooked through. Serve hot with the chutney.

Chef's tip To make chile oil, warm 2 cups vegetable oil.
Add 3 dried chiles. Remove from the heat and infuse for
24 hours, then strain into a sterilized bottle and store for
up to 2 months in a cool, dark place. Refrigerate in
warmer climates.

Lamb medallions with cilantro sauce

Toasted pine nuts add a wonderful texture to these medallions of pink lamb, presented on a bed of spinach, with a syrupy sauce of shallots and herbs.

Preparation time **30 minutes**
Total cooking time **30 minutes**
Serves 4

2 x 6–7-chop lamb rib roasts
1 tablespoon oil or clarified butter
2 large shallots, chopped
2 cups lamb stock (see page 62)
   or light beef stock
1/2 cup chopped fresh cilantro leaves
1 tablespoon chopped fresh mint leaves
1 tablespoon hazelnut oil
3 lb. young spinach leaves, picked over
   and washed
2 large tomatoes, peeled, seeded and diced into
   1/4-inch cubes
2/3 cup pine nuts (pignoli), toasted

1 Remove the "eye" or long round tenderloin of meat at the thick end of each rack by running a small, sharp knife along the bone. Trim off the fat and sinew.
2 Heat the oil or clarified butter in a skillet. Season the lamb with salt, then fry over gentle heat, turning now and then, for 10–12 minutes, or until still just pink inside, yet browned outside. Remove the lamb from the pan; keep warm and set aside to rest.
3 Drain the pan of any excess fat, then add the shallots and cook for about 2 minutes, or until lightly colored. Add the stock, bring to a boil, then reduce the heat and simmer rapidly for about 10 minutes, or until the mixture is syrupy. Remove from the heat, adjust the seasoning, then stir in the cilantro and mint. Cover and keep warm.
4 In another skillet, heat the hazelnut oil and quickly cook the whole spinach leaves over high heat until just wilted. Drain and season to taste with salt and pepper. Pack the spinach into four flat 1-cup molds or ramekins, then turn each mold out onto the center of a warm plate.
5 Carve the lamb into medallions about 1/4-inch thick. Arrange the medallions on the spinach beds and swirl the sauce around; sprinkle the chopped tomatoes and pine nuts over the sauce. Roasted potatoes are a wonderful accompaniment.

Chef's tip Ask your butcher to remove the tenderloins from the racks of lamb for you.

Chilled melon soup
with eau-de-Cologne mint sorbet

While working at a hotel in the Channel Islands, a chef encountered an eau-de-Cologne mint growing in a walled garden. He was inspired to try the mint in a sorbet, and his wonderful creation became popularly known at the hotel as "Sorbet 4711."

Preparation time **15 minutes + 2 hours refrigeration**
  + churning
Total cooking time **5 minutes**
Serves 4

I musk melon, such as cantaloupe, Persian, Crenshaw
  or honeydew
2 lb. watermelon, peeled and chopped
1/2 cup sugar
3/4 cup finely chopped eau-de-Cologne mint
  (see Chef's tips)
juice of I lemon, or to taste

1 To make the melon soup, halve the musk melon and remove the seeds. Scoop the flesh into a blender or food processor with the flesh from the watermelon (you don't need to remove the seeds). Process to a purée, then rub through a strainer into a bowl to remove the watermelon seeds. If the melons are slightly under-ripe you may need to add sugar or lemon juice to develop the flavor. Cover and refrigerate for 2 hours.

2 To make the mint sorbet, gently heat the sugar and 2 cups water in a small saucepan and stir to dissolve the sugar. Bring to a boil, then remove from the heat and allow to cool. Add the mint and lemon juice to taste.
3 Pour the syrup into an ice-cream machine and churn until firm. (The churning time will vary depending on your machine.)
4 Ladle the soup into chilled bowls and spoon the sorbet into the center. Serve immediately.

Chef's tips Eau-de-Cologne mint is also known as orange mint, but regular spearmint may also be used.

  If you do not have an ice-cream machine, pour the mixture into a shallow metal container, freeze until crystals form, then whisk or stir with a fork and return to the freezer. Repeat until frozen evenly and firm.

  As it is difficult to make a small quantity of sorbet, you will have some left over. Serve it between courses to cleanse the palate, or to accompany fruit, dessert or chocolate. The sorbet may be frozen in an airtight container for up to 1 week, but it is best served freshly made if possible.

Strawberries Romanoff

Deceptively easy to prepare, this memorable dessert will leave a lasting impression on your guests. Orange juice may be used in place of the liqueur.

*Preparation time **15 minutes + overnight refrigeration
+ 30 minutes chilling***
*Total cooking time **10 minutes***
Serves 6

3/4 lb. fresh strawberries
1/4 cup sugar
3 tablespoons Kirsch or Grand Marnier
1 3/4 cups heavy cream
a few drops of vanilla extract
2 tablespoons strained apricot jam
2/3 cup chopped good-quality semisweet chocolate
rose leaves, washed and dried (optional)

1 Wash and thoroughly dry the strawberries and set three aside for decoration. Remove the stems from the remaining strawberries. Coarsely chop the fruit, place in a bowl and add the sugar and liqueur. Toss well, cover with plastic wrap and refrigerate overnight.

2 Mix the cream and vanilla and whisk lightly using a balloon whisk until the whisk just leaves a trail, yet the cream still runs if the bowl is tilted. Add half the strawberries and whisk to a firm peak. Spoon the mixture into a pastry bag without a nozzle.

3 Place the remaining strawberries into six 3/4-cup serving glasses. Pipe the cream mixture onto the strawberries, to reach just below the rim of the glasses. Transfer to the refrigerator and chill for 30 minutes.

4 Bring the jam and 2 teaspoons water to a boil in a small saucepan. Slice the reserved strawberries in half, through the stem. Brush the cut-side of each strawberry with the melted glaze and set aside to cool. Decorate each glass with a strawberry half.

5 Place the chocolate in the top of a double boiler over hot water and stir gently until the chocolate has melted. Brush a thick layer of chocolate onto the shiny side of each rose leaf, then gently place on a plate lined with waxed paper and refrigerate for 5 minutes to allow the chocolate to set.

6 To serve, carefully peel the leaves from the paper and place a chocolate leaf on each chilled dessert.

Chef's tips Any fresh berries which are in season may be used in this recipe.

For a family dinner, you can make the dessert in a large glass serving bowl. Or to finish off a very elegant dinner-party, you could serve the Romanoff in store-bought chocolate cups or cookie tulipes.

Blueberry and buttermilk sorbet

This refreshing sorbet is a perfect palate refresher after a heavy meal. The buttermilk provides a tangy contrast to the sweet, juicy blueberries.

Preparation time **15 minutes + churning**
Total cooking time **5 minutes**
Serves 4

☼

3/4 lb. fresh blueberries
1/2 cup sugar
I cup buttermilk
juice of I lemon, or to taste
I egg white

1 Place the blueberries, sugar and ½ cup water in a saucepan. Stir over medium heat until the sugar dissolves. Bring to a boil, remove from the heat and allow to cool slightly. Using a metal or wooden spoon, press the mixture through a metal strainer to make a pulp, discarding the contents of the strainer. Alternatively, purée the mixture in a food processor, then press the pulp through a strainer.

2 Stir the buttermilk into the fruit pulp and add the lemon juice. In a separate bowl, lightly whisk the egg white with a fork until frothy, then stir into the blueberry and buttermilk mixture. Transfer to an ice-cream machine and churn until frozen and smooth. Serve immediately in chilled glasses.

Chef's tips If you do not have an ice-cream machine, pour the mixture into a shallow metal container, freeze until crystals form, then whisk or stir with a fork and return to the freezer. Repeat until frozen evenly and firm.

This sorbet is best enjoyed on the day it is made, but will also freeze for up to 1 week in an airtight container.

Any berries may be substituted for the blueberries, or you could use a combination of berries to make a "fruits of the forest" buttermilk sorbet. Frozen berries may also be substituted: defrost and drain before use.

For a chunkier sorbet, lightly break up the fruit with a fork in step 1, instead of using a strainer.

Lemon sabayon
with fresh berries

The name of this superb dessert is derived from the French word for zabaglione. *Like a true* zabaglione, *a sabayon is best served on the day it is made.*

*Preparation time **45 minutes + 1 hour refrigeration***
*Total cooking time **25 minutes***
*Serves **4–6***

SABAYON
3 eggs
¹/2 cup sugar
¹/3 cup lemon juice
¹/3 cup unsalted butter, softened

I cup raspberries
I cup blueberries
I cup blackberries
¹/3 cup confectioners' sugar
4 sprigs of fresh mint, to decorate

1 To make the sabayon, half fill a large saucepan with water and heat until simmering. Have ready a heatproof bowl that will fit over the pan without touching the water. Place the eggs, sugar and lemon juice in the bowl and place it over the simmering water. With a whisk or an electric mixer, beat until foamy, then constantly beat for 20–25 minutes, or until the mixture is thick and light yellow and leaves a trail as it falls from the whisk or beaters.

2 Remove the bowl from the heat and whisk in the butter, a teaspoon at a time. Strain into a bowl placed over ice, then whisk for 15 minutes, or until very cold. Remove from the ice and chill for at least 1 hour, or until ready to serve.

3 Set aside the four nicest berries of each type of fruit; toss the rest with the confectioners' sugar. Fill the bottom quarter of four large wine glasses or champagne flutes with sabayon, then spoon some fruit on top. Cover with a second layer of sabayon and fruit, finishing with a final layer of sabayon. Arrange the reserved berries on top and garnish with a sprig of mint. Chill until ready to serve.

Fraisier

This is a wonderful cake for an elegant picnic, or to end a light summer meal. If pink marzipan is not available, knead a few drops of red food coloring through the marzipan until the color is uniform.

Preparation time **1 hour 50 minutes + cooling**
Total cooking time **40 minutes**
Serves 6–8

✦ ✦ ✦

GENOESE SPONGE
3 eggs
I egg yolk
1/2 cup sugar
I cup all-purpose flour
I tablespoon unsalted butter, melted and cooled

SYRUP
1/3 cup sugar
2 tablespoons Kirsch

CREME MOUSSELINE
I cup milk
I vanilla bean
1/4 cup sugar
2 egg yolks
3 tablespoons all-purpose flour
3 tablespoons cornstarch
I tablespoon Kirsch
1/2 cup unsalted butter, softened

3 1/3 cups strawberries, hulled
2 1/2 tablespoons strained strawberry jam
3 oz. pink marzipan

1 Preheat the oven to 350°F. To make the Genoese sponge, whisk or beat the eggs, egg yolk and sugar in a heatproof bowl over a saucepan of hot steaming water until it leaves a trail. Remove from the heat and whisk until cold. Sift the flour, fold it into the mixture, then fold in the melted butter. Pour into a lightly greased 8-inch springform pan and bake for 20–25 minutes, or until the cake shrinks from the side of the pan. Run a knife inside the ring to release the cake, then cool on a wire rack. Cut the cold cake horizontally in half.

2 To make the syrup, dissolve the sugar in 1/4 cup water in a small saucepan over low heat. Bring to a boil and boil for 1 minute, then stir in the Kirsch.

3 To make the crème mousseline, bring the milk and vanilla bean to a boil. In a bowl, whisk the sugar and egg yolks until pale, then stir in the flour and cornstarch. Strain the milk into the yolk mixture, whisking constantly. Return the mixture to the pan and stir rapidly over medium heat until thickened, then boil for 1 minute, stirring constantly. Remove from the heat to cool completely. Add the Kirsch and gradually beat in the butter, whisking well between each addition.

4 Set aside a strawberry for decoration. Halve a third of the strawberries and quarter the rest. To assemble, place a cake layer in the clean, dry springform ring (placed on a flat plate), baked-side-down. Brush with some syrup, spread with a little jam and some of the mousseline. Place the halved strawberries around the outer edge of the cake, the cut sides facing out.

5 Spoon the mousseline into a pastry bag fitted with a 1/2-inch nozzle. Pipe into the gaps between the strawberries. Arrange the remaining strawberries over the cake, then cover with the remaining mousseline. Smooth the surface and gently press the other cake layer on top.

6 Remove the springform ring. Brush on more syrup and thinly spread with jam. Dust a work area with confectioners' sugar, roll out the marzipan to a 1/8-inch thick circle, and cut a circle with the springform ring. Lift the marzipan onto the cake and smooth the top. Heat the remaining jam, dip in the whole strawberry and place it on top of the cake.

Gratin of summer berries

Beneath a luscious froth of sabayon, quickly broiled until golden brown, lies an assortment of fresh, sweet berries for a delectable summer dessert.

*Preparation time **20 minutes***
*Total cooking time **20 minutes***
Serves 4

2³/4 cups mixed berries, such as strawberries,
    blueberries, raspberries and blackberries
2 eggs
2 egg yolks
5 tablespoons sugar
I tablespoon Kirsch

1 Wash the strawberries, dry well, discard the stems and cut each strawberry in half. Sort the remaining berries to make sure they are all fresh. Arrange the fruit on four ovenproof plates or individual shallow dishes.

2 Half fill a large saucepan with water and heat until simmering. Have ready a heatproof bowl that will fit over the pan without actually touching the water.

3 To make the sabayon, place the eggs, egg yolks, sugar and Kirsch in the bowl, then place the bowl over the pan of simmering water, making sure the base of the bowl is not touching the water. Whisk or beat with an electric mixer for 10–15 minutes, or until the mixture is thick and creamy and leaves a trail as it falls from the whisk or beaters.

4 Preheat the broiler to high. Spoon the sabayon over the berries and quickly broil until the sabayon is brown all over. Serve immediately.

Chef's tip The plates of fruit can be arranged in advance, but cover with plastic wrap so they do not dry out.

Chef's techniques

Making lamb stock

Ask your butcher to chop the lamb bones so they will fit in your saucepan.

 Put 3 lb. of lamb bones in a large stockpot. Cover with water and bring to a boil. Drain and rinse the bones.

 Return the bones to a clean saucepan and add 1 quartered onion, 2 carrots, 1 leek and 1 celery stalk, all chopped, as well as 3 quarts of water, 1 bouquet garni and 6 peppercorns.

 Bring to a boil, reduce the heat and simmer for 2–3 hours, skimming the fat and scum from the surface regularly. A flat strainer is easiest to use for skimming.

 Ladle the bones and vegetables into a fine strainer over a bowl. Press the bones and vegetables with the ladle to extract all the liquid. Refrigerate for several hours and remove the solidified fat. Makes about 6 cups.

Boning a leg and thigh

Tunnel boning, shown here, creates a pocket in one end, which is also ideal for holding a stuffing.

 Starting at the thigh end and using a sharp knife, find the thigh bone and run the point of the knife along the top and inside of the bone to release the meat.

 Continue down along the bone, scraping down and around to the joint: the meat will gradually turn inside out. Ease the meat off the joint, pulling the boned meat back firmly, being careful not to cut through to the skin.

 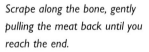 Scrape along the bone, gently pulling the meat back until you reach the end.

 Holding the bone and meat firmly, pull hard to remove the bone. You may need the knife to help release any tough tendons. Turn the meat inside out to its original shape.

Removing lobster tail meat

This simple technique makes it easy to present the lobster tail meat in neat, elegant portions.

Turn the lobster on its tail. Using a pair of kitchen scissors, cut lengthwise down each side of the belly.

Pull the soft undershell back, exposing the meat of the lobster tail.

Pull the tail meat from the shell, keeping it in a single piece.

Preparing a crab

This method can be used on most crabs. Mud crab, shown here, needs extra care as the shell is very hard.

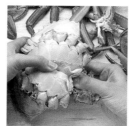

Twist the claws to remove them. Use your thumb as a lever to prise off the hard top shell. Scoop out any creamy brown meat and reserve. Wash and dry the shell well.

Discard the soft stomach sac from the main body of the crab and remove the grey spongy fingers (gills). Scrape out and reserve any more creamy brown meat.

Cut the main body of the crab in half lengthwise, then remove the white meat from the body using the end of a teaspoon or fork.

Tying asparagus

Tying a bunch of asparagus makes it easier to handle during cooking.

Grasp the aparagus bunch in the center. Holding the end of a string with thumb and finger, wrap the string around the upper part three times, cross over and wrap the lower part three times. Secure with a knot.

Bouquet garni

Add the flavor and aroma of herbs to your dish with a freshly made bouquet garni.

Wrap the green part of a leek loosely around a bay leaf, a sprig of thyme, some celery leaves and a few stalks of parsley, then tie with string. Leave a long tail to the string for easy removal.

First published in the United States in 1998 by Periplus Editions (HK) Ltd., with editorial offices at
153 Milk Street, Boston, Massachusetts 02109.

Murdoch Books and Le Cordon Bleu thank the 32 masterchefs of all the Le Cordon Bleu Schools, whose knowledge and
expertise have made this book possible, especially: Chef Cliche (MOF), Chef Terrien, Chef Boucheret, Chef Duchêne (MOF),
Chef Guillut, Chef Steneck, Paris; Chef Males, Chef Walsh, Chef Hardy, London; Chef Chantefort, Chef Bertin, Chef Jambert,
Chef Honda, Tokyo; Chef Salembien, Chef Boutin, Chef Harris, Sydney; Chef Lawes, Adelaide; Chef Guiet, Chef Denis, Ottawa.
Of the many students who helped the Chefs test each recipe, a special mention to graduates David Welch and Allen Wertheim.
A very special acknowledgment to Directors Susan Eckstein, Great Britain, and Kathy Shaw, Paris, who have been responsible for
the coordination of the Le Cordon Bleu team throughout this series.

The Publisher and Le Cordon Bleu also wish to thank Carole Sweetnam for her help with this series.

First published in Australia in 1998 by Murdoch Books®

Managing Editor: Kay Halsey
Series Concept, Design and Art Direction: Juliet Cohen
Editor: Katri Hilden
Food Director: Jody Vassallo
Food Editor: Dimitra Stais
US Editor: Linda Venturoni Wilson
Designer: Wing Ping Tong
Photographer: Joe Filshie
Food Stylist: Carolyn Fienberg
Food Preparation: Jo Forrest
Chef's Techniques Photographer: Reg Morrison
Home Economists: Michelle Earl, Michelle Lawton, Kerrie Mullins, Justine Poole, Kerrie Ray, Margot Smithyman

Library of Congress catalog card number: 98-85726
ISBN 962-593-450-2

Front cover: Salade niçoise

Distributed in the United States by
Charles E. Tuttle Co., Inc.
RR1 Box 231-5
North Clarendon, VT 05759
Tel: (802) 773-8930
Fax: (802) 773-6993

PRINTED IN SINGAPORE

05 04 03 02 01 00 99 98 10 9 8 7 6 5 4 3 2 1

Important: Some of the recipes in this book may include raw eggs, which can cause salmonella poisoning.
Those who might be at risk from this (the elderly, pregnant women, young children and those suffering
from immune deficiency diseases) should check with their physicians before eating raw eggs.